# CONTENTS

2  Spot the Difference

4  Answers to Spot the Difference

5  Get Wombat Home

6  Bookmarks

7  Echidna's Maze

8  Mobile

9  Sticker Action; Mystery Word; How to Assemble Your Bushlands Diorama

10  Bushlands Diorama

11  Giant Crossword

12  Bushlands Adventure Board Game

14  Word Search

16  Fly Your Own Kite

19  Where am I?

20  Who am I?

21  Game Cards

23  Doorhangers

24  Grow Your Own Gum Tree

Inside back cover - Answers

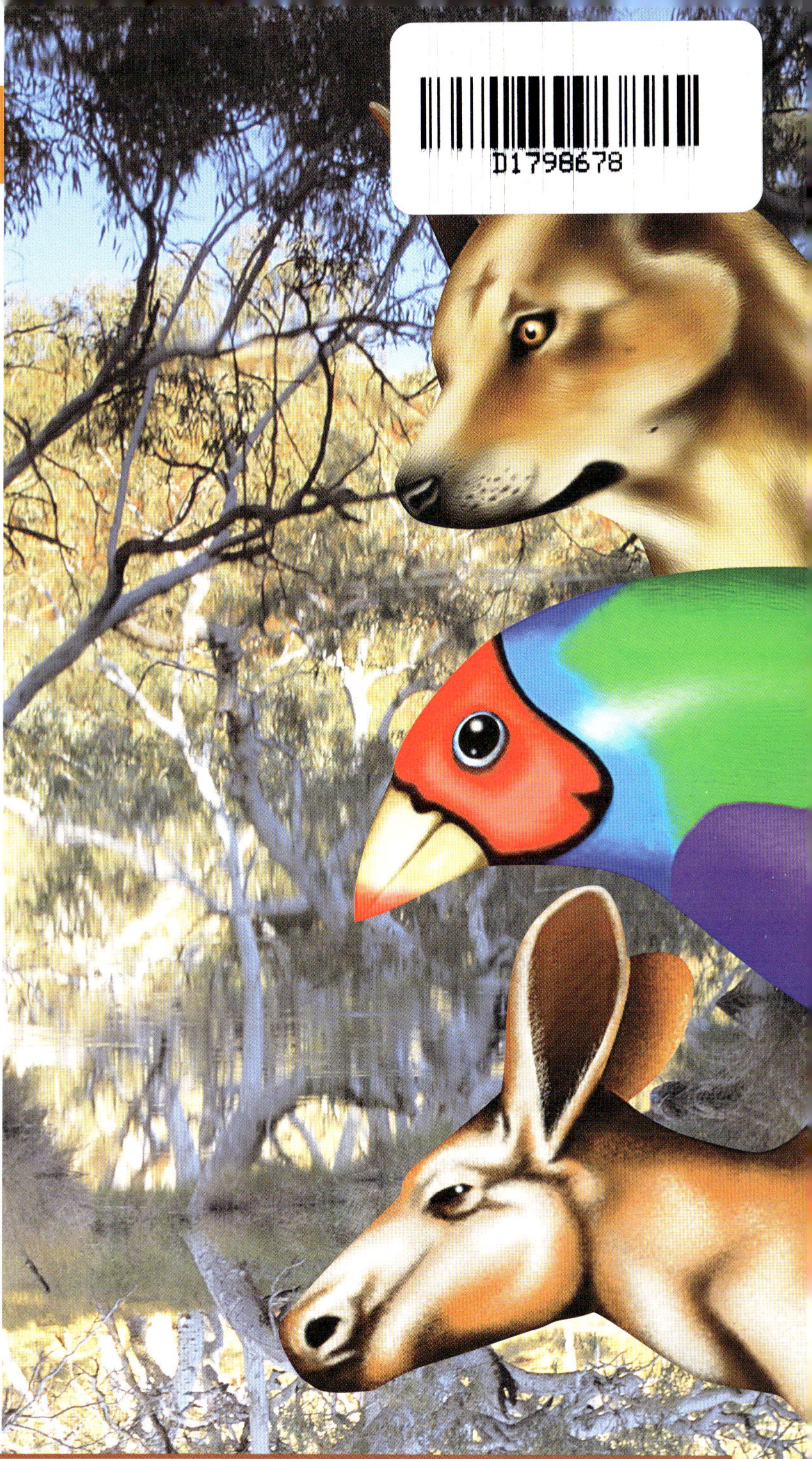

## How to Use this Book

Before you start your bushlands fun here are some things you will need to know:

- Look for the symbols. They tell you what you need for each activity.
- Stop when you see this symbol. Look on the back of the page before you start cutting.
- The Stickers, Board Game, Diorama and Mobile are on double pages in the middle of the book. You will have to pull out these pages carefully.
- Remember to ask for help if you need it.

Now you're ready to have some fun!

## THINGS YOU WILL NEED

 LOOK AT BACK OF PAGE FIRST

 GLUE

 PAPER OR CARDBOARD

 PENCILS

 SCISSORS

There are ten things on this page that are different from the picture on page 2. The differences are in each animal or group of animals.

3

# Answers to Spot the Difference

The ten differences between the pictures on pages 2 and 3 are circled below.

## DINGO

The Dingo has sensitive, upright ears. The ear shape and fringing hairs help channel sound into the ear. This predator's ears can twist sideways to follow noises.

## FRILLED LIZARD

This reptile raises its neck frill to frighten predators. The male also waves his frill to attract females and warn other males to stay out of his territory.

## TIGER SNAKE

A tiger snake's forked tongue tastes the air for smells. The tongue has no poison or sting. The poison is injected through the hollow fangs on its top jaw.

## BILBY

The Bilby was a common marsupial in Australia's grassy woodlands until about 1900. Today this endangered bandicoot is found only in the central deserts.

## GOULDIAN FINCHES

The Gouldian Finch's head can be black, red or yellow. Black is the most common head colour. Yellow-headed birds are very rare.

## GALAH

Galahs are usually found in flocks. Feeding in flocks enables the birds to locate the food more effectively and share the findings. It also means that, with so many eyes to keep a lookout, there is greater protection from predators.

## WEDGE-TAILED EAGLE

This bird has a strong, hooked bill for tearing up its food. The Wedge-tailed Eagle eats mammals, reptiles and birds. It is Australia's largest bird of prey.

## EMU

This fast moving bird has long, powerful legs. It also has wings but cannot fly. The Emu travels far to find enough seeds, flowers, grass shoots and insects.

## RED KANGAROOS

A kangaroo uses its large tail as a prop when standing and to balance when hopping. To move slowly, the kangaroo leans on its tail and front legs, then swings its hind legs forward.

## NUMBAT

As the Numbat is a daytime animal, the dark stripes on its body probably serve as a form of camouflage known as disruptive coloration. This means that when the animal is moving through the bush, the shape of the Numbat blurs and it is difficult for predators to see it clearly.

# Get Wombat Home

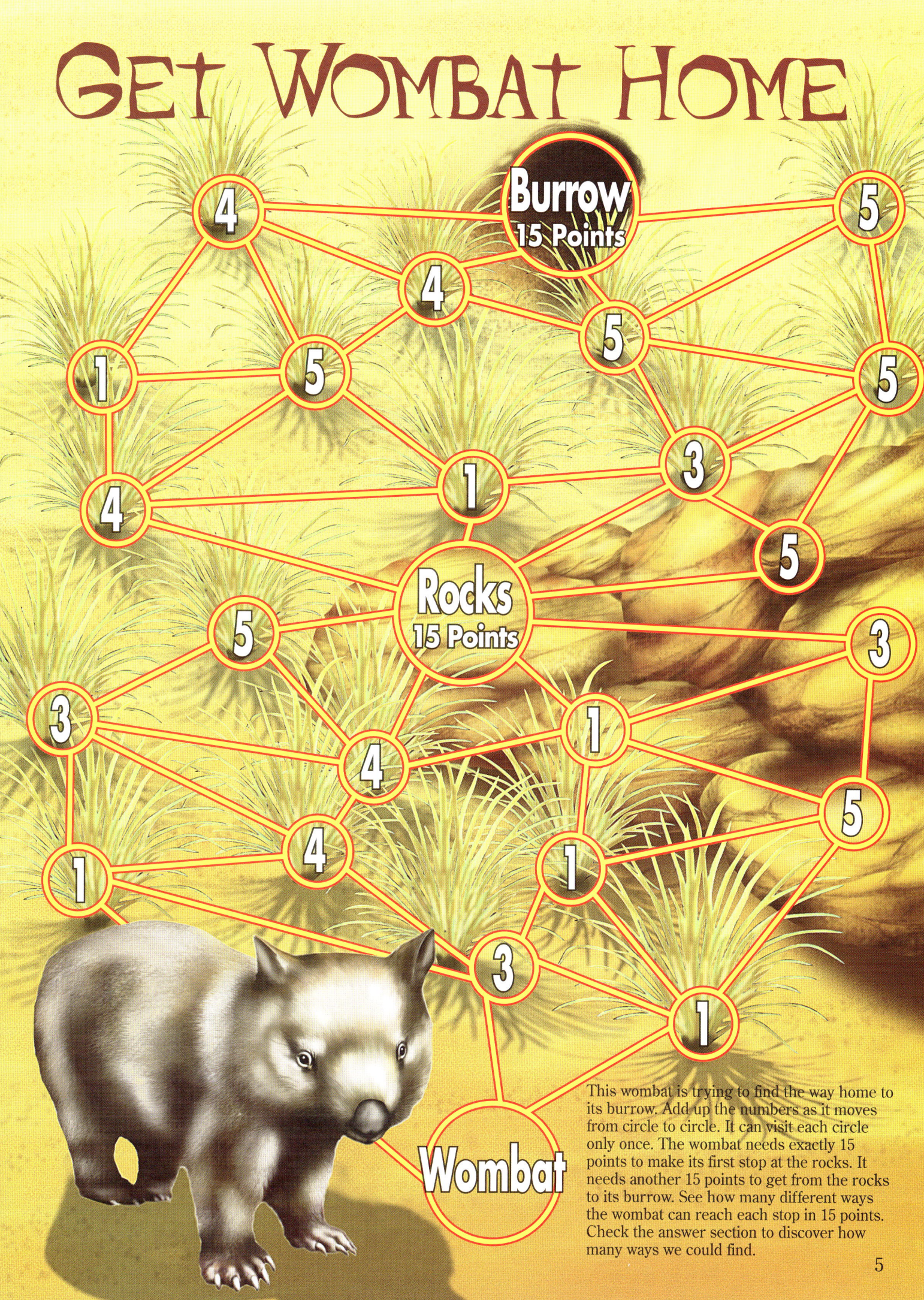

This wombat is trying to find the way home to its burrow. Add up the numbers as it moves from circle to circle. It can visit each circle only once. The wombat needs exactly 15 points to make its first stop at the rocks. It needs another 15 points to get from the rocks to its burrow. See how many different ways the wombat can reach each stop in 15 points. Check the answer section to discover how many ways we could find.

# Bookmarks

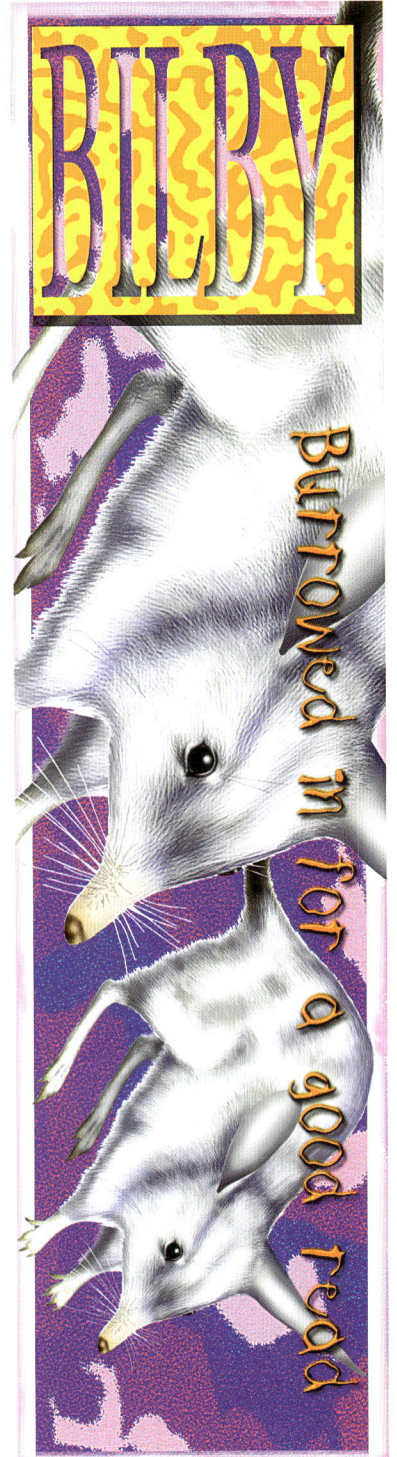

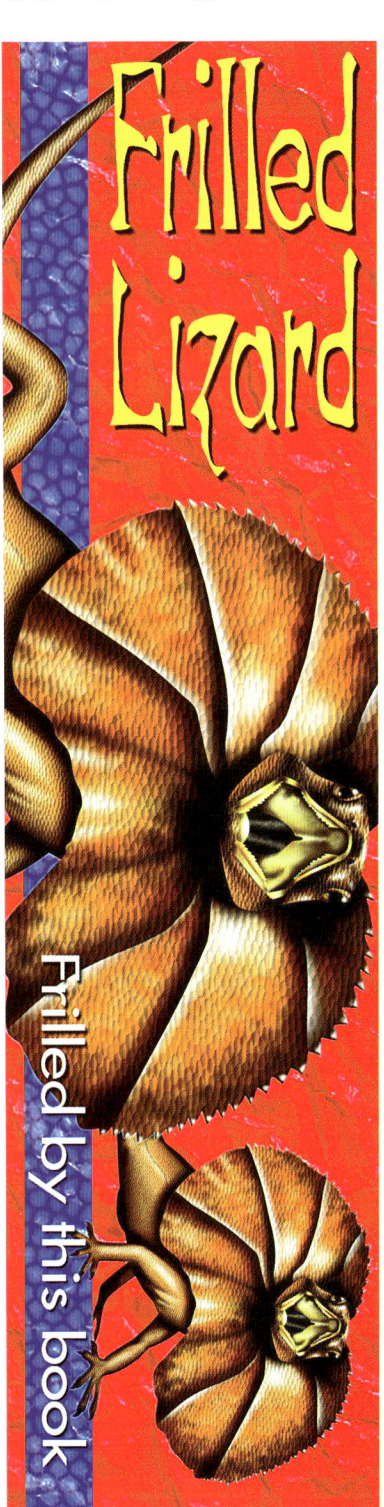

## The Bilby

Bilbies dig burrows up to 3 metres long, and this is where they spend the whole day, emerging to feed only at night.

## Frilled Lizard

The Frilled Lizard opens its frill to scare away possible attackers. Perhaps it can guard the pages of one of your books.

## Create your own

Here's your chance to be creative. Use a plant or animal in this book for inspiration. Try a drawing or a poem. Don't forget your bushlands stickers.

# Echidna's Maze

**DID YOU KNOW**

The echidna's favourite food is ants and termites. An echidna has no teeth, so it crushes its food between horny plates on its tongue and the roof of its mouth.

Help the echidna's tongue find the ant inside the nest.

Start here...

# Mobile (front)

STOP

FOLD HERE

## HOW TO ASSEMBLE

1 Lift out page. Cut along the dotted line at the top to remove the head banner (A).

2 Paste a length of thin cardboard over the back of A.

3 Cut a piece of thin cardboard half the size of B and put glue on both sides. Lay it on one half of the back of B, then fold the other half of B back on to the cardboard.

## STICKER ACTION

There are a thousand things you can do with stickers. You could use them in this book to bring your bushlands diorama to life or decorate a bookmark.

**Why not USE them to:**
- manufacture a mobile
- tattoo your torso
- plaster a postcard
- beautify your bike
- decorate your dog's collar
- brighten up a birthday card

# Mystery Word

Use the animal clues to solve the crossword puzzle. Then unscramble the circled letters to find the mystery word.

# How to assemble your bushlands Diorama

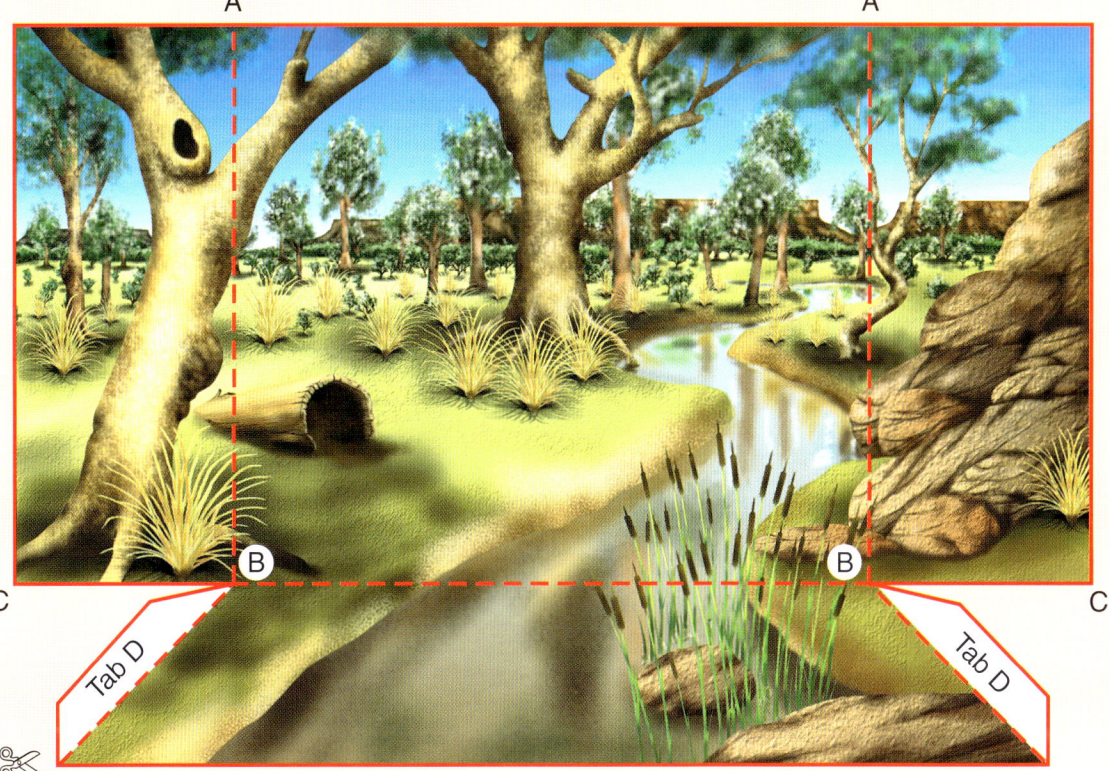

**1** Remove diorama from book. Glue it onto a piece of cardboard.

**2** Cut out diorama. Cut carefully around Tab D and from C to B. Do not cut past B.

**3** Fold towards centre each side section along A to B. Open out sides.

**4** Fold bottom section upwards along B to B. Open out again.

**5** Fold each Tab D inwards, then open out. Glue front of Tab D to back of diorama between C and B.

A

C

B

STOP

Tab D

# Giant Crossword

## ACROSS

1. Short for Budgerigar.
3. Has wings but cannot fly.
4. Many animals do this when thirsty.
6. A common possum.
8. Many insects live in rotting _ _ _ _.
9. Has huge feet and hops.
11. Spiny anteater.
13. Sleepy gum leaf eater.
14. A cockatoo raises this when alarmed.
15. Food for echidnas.
19. A bird of prey.
21. Lives in tree hollows and roofs.
23. Some birds do this when they stay in the air in one place.
25. A black spider with a bright colour on its back.
26. A cat-sized native animal with spots.

## DOWN

1. A type of habitat.
2. A group of kangaroos.
4. Australia's native dog.
5. A laughing bird.
7. A nectar-eating bird.
8. A mammal that digs long tunnels.
10. This lizard is sometimes called a monitor.
11. A gum tree.
12. Six-legged food for many animals.
16. Has a forked tongue.
17. A pink and grey parrot.
18. Has a bushy tail and sticky tongue.
20. A keen sense of this helps an animal to locate food.
22. A tree grows from this.
24. A silent night-hunter.

Decide to pick a native flower.
Lose all your cards.

Disturb a Malleefowl nesting mound.
Lose two cards.

Frightened by a howling Dingo.
Lose two cards.

snake.

Stop to let a tiger snake
cross your path.
Pick up a card.

You have helped an injured glider.
Pick up the rest of the cards.

Spot a Koala up a gum tree.
Pick up a card.

Bush
ADVE

Tasmanian Devil scares you.
Lose a card.

Chase a butterfly.
Pick up a card.

Watch a bee-eater de-sting a bee.
Pick up a card.

FINISH

Watch an echidna make a burrow.
Pick up a card.

START

FRILLED

TO BE HERE

Leave Koalas some trees

BILBIES 'Not Bushlands'

What a Galah

ALWAYS HAVE TIME FOR A LAUGH KOOKABURRAS

Leave bushlands for the birds

DON'T MESS WITH ME I'M A THORNY DEVIL

Hello Possums

This book belongs to:

GO JUMP

ands

TURE

This is a game for two or more players. On pages 22–23 you will find the Australian animal facts cards. Cut these out and place them on this square. You will need one dice and one small item to use as a counter for each player - anything will do, buttons, erasers, paper clips, it's up to you. Place your counters on START and proceed around the board, collecting cards as you go. The player with the most cards at the FINISH wins. In the event of a tie between two players, take turns in rolling the dice. Roll an odd number, lose a card to the other player; roll an even, keep your cards. Continue until one person has no more cards.

Watch a bandicoot. Pick up.

Accidentally trip over a Numbat. Lose a card.

Watch a Thorny Devil change colours. Pick up a card.

Stung by a Scorpion. Lose two cards.

See a soaring Wedge-tailed Eagle. Pick up two cards.

Disturb a colony of endangered Bilbies. Pick up two cards.

Chased by an Emu. Lose a card.

Hear a kookaburra laugh. Pick up a card.

ob of kangaroos. e a card.

Find a wombat burrow. Pick up a card.

Frightened a Frilled Lizard. Lose a card.

# Word Search

The bushland words listed below are hidden in this puzzle. How many can you find?

```
E W B U Q U O L L M D L G K G H
U C Z Y E I N A L E M I Z X E R
C X H P A B E E T L E O N M C E
A D R I Y Z R K A T P A M G K D
L W E J D A L D A T Z O K L O I
Y O V A C N G R N N X N S O Y L
P M E K P G A H R S S V R S C G
T V L O E Z Y L R Z X A K S U V
A G O A N N A M B L G U Z K B M
F B H L M D Q E F N I E M I C H
B R K A A E K S A T X N P N F K
E S O E L M J K A B V U U K R G
K G Q G E L Z B W D T M D O W L
Y S W H X S P I D E R B G I O D
B U T T E R F L Y N C A U P M A
A C O J W B U C X Z L T V B B R
L D E F S E I T H A V M I L A R
L Q S Z B R A L H O I U B G T U
A Y A N X N M G B A R N O P L B
W A R A T A H U L Y F Y E M U A
X Z E P E U C T M E B J K P T K
P G S W R E N Y E T I M R E T O
Y A I B M G O L L I Z A R D A O
W A T T L E M F W Y E W O H L K
```

BEETLE
BILBY
BUTTERFLY
DINGO
EAGLE
ECHIDNA
EMU
EUCALYPT
FROG
(GALAH)
GECKO
GLIDER
GOANNA
KANGAROO
KOALA
KOOKABURRA
LIZARD
NUMBAT
OWL
POSSUM
QUOLL
SKINK
SNAKE
SPIDER
TERMITE
WALLABY
WARATAH
WASP
WATTLE
WOMBAT
WREN

14

A

B

C

STOP

Tab D

15

# Fly your own Kite

**You will also need:**
- 1 piece of paper 74 x 74 cm
- 1 stick 72 cm
- 1 stick 54 cm
  (both sticks should be about 2cm wide and flat on one side)
- string, glue and scissors
- poster paints or coloured pens

HINTS:

This kite doesn't have a tail, but you may need to attach a short one if the kite is too unsteady.

An empty plastic bottle makes a good reel for your kite line.

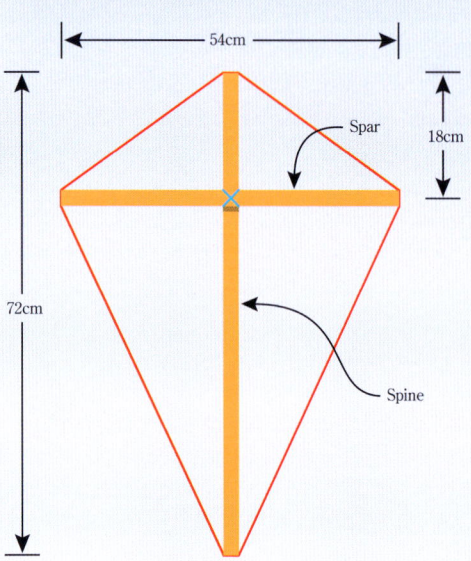

## 1 The Frame

Carefully notch the end of each stick for the frame string. Mark the centre of the short stick (the spar).

Measure and mark 18 cm from one end of the long stick (the spine).

Glue the flat side of the sticks together at these marks and tie with string.

Cut a 2 m long piece of string. Fit the string around the frame guiding it along the notches.

Tie both ends around the bottom.

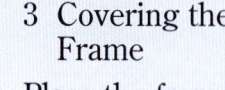

## 3 Covering the Frame

Place the frame on the back of the cover so the frame string matches the fold lines. Glue the flaps over the string.

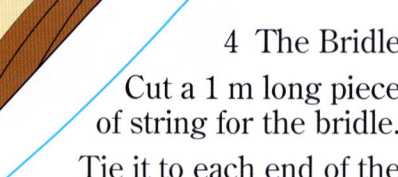

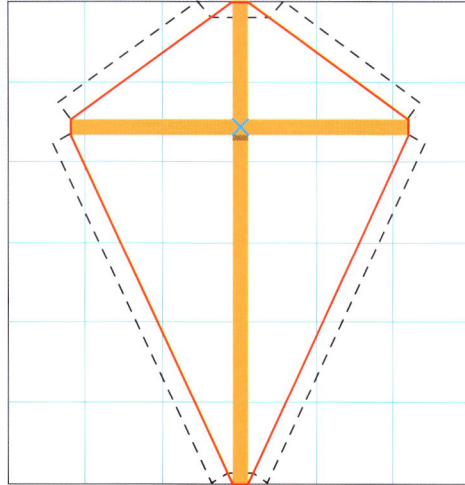

## 2 The Cover

Draw a grid on your paper. Centre the frame on the grid.

Use a ruler to help you draw the fold lines and flaps. The frame string should match the fold lines.

Take the frame off the paper.

Sketch in the owl using the grid lines. Colour the owl and cut out the cover.

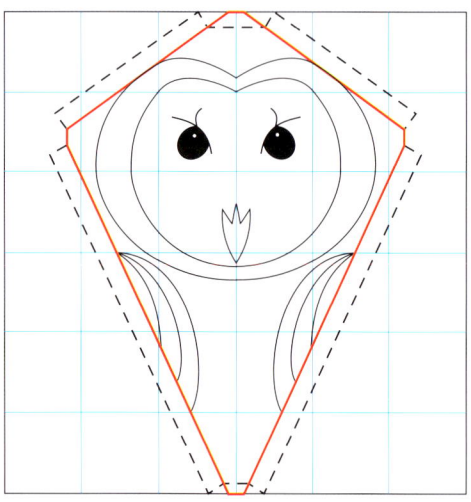

## 4 The Bridle

Cut a 1 m long piece of string for the bridle.

Tie it to each end of the spine below the frame string. Measure and mark the bridle line 20 cm from the top.

Attach the bridle to your kite line at this mark. You may need to adjust this.

16

STOP | GLUE | | ✂

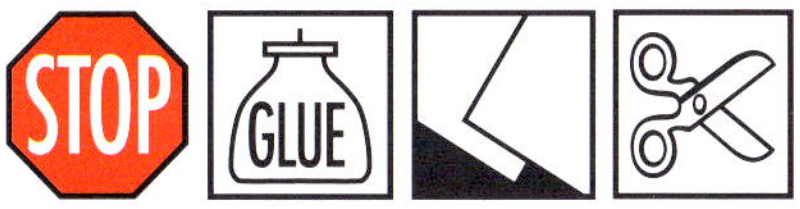

## BUSHLANDS MOBILE

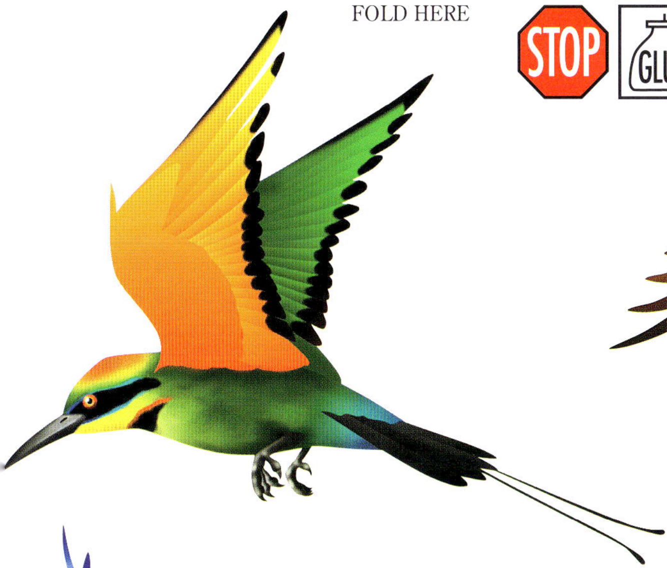

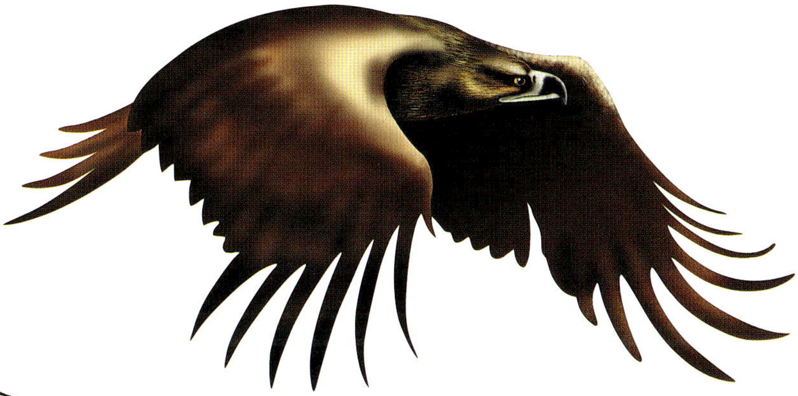

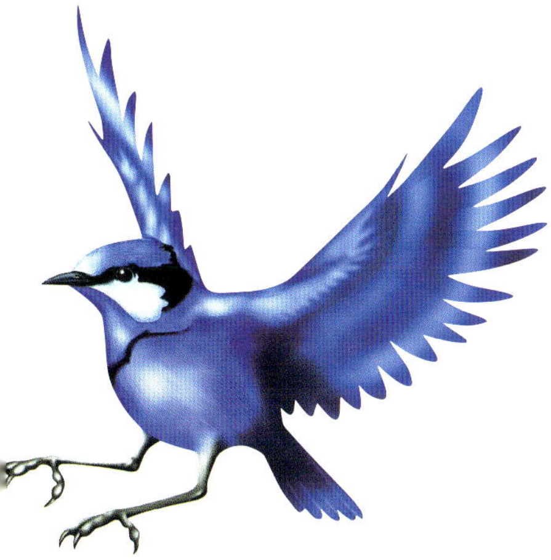

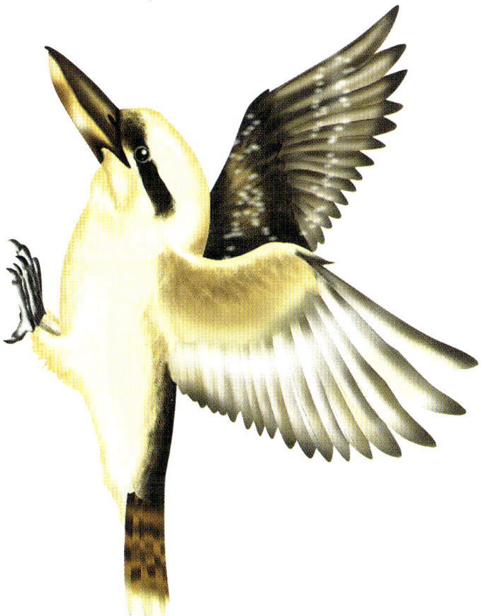

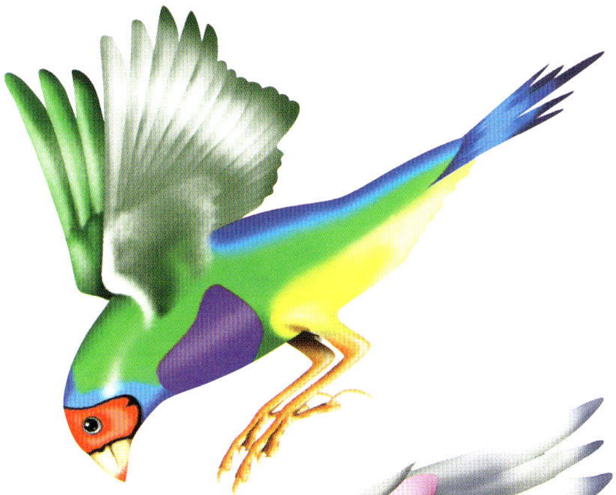

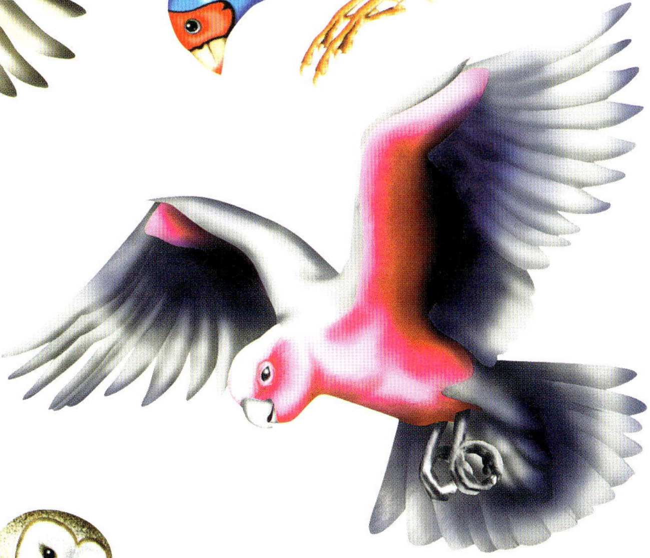

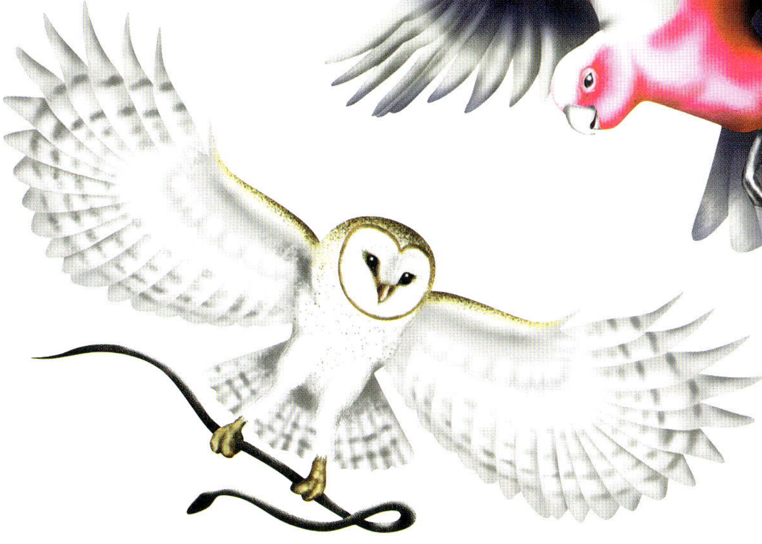

ld A at the dotted
es and glue to
a triangle.

t out the 7
shlands birds
the blue line.

6 Poke holes at the red
dots. Cut 10 lengths of
string, assemble the
mobile, and knot the ends
of the strings.

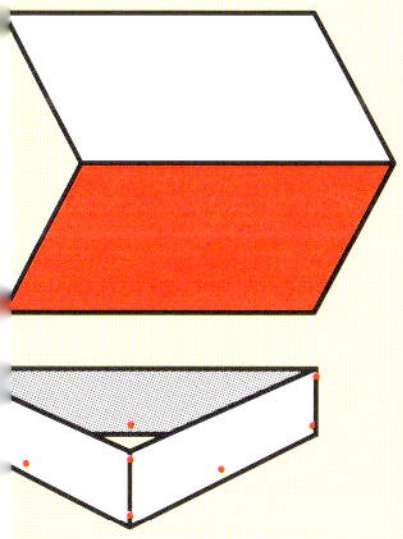

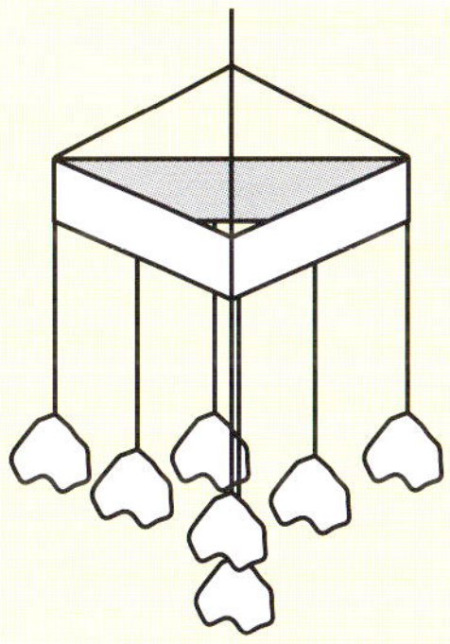

# Where am I?

There are many types of bushlands throughout Australia, and these different habitats provide food and shelter for a variety of interesting animals.

Can you find where these bushlands animals are hiding?

1. Brushtail possum
2. Sugar Glider
3. Koala and baby
4. Kookaburra
5. Splendid Fairy-wren
6. Numbat
7. Frilled Lizard
8. Bluetongue Lizard
9. Tiger snake
10. Tasmanian Devil
11. Echidna
12. Dingo
13. Koala
14. Red Kangaroo
15. Galah
16. Rainbow Bee-eater
17. Malleefowl

# Who am I?

See if you can identify this bushlands animal. Here are some clues:
- I spend most of my time sleeping and eating.
- I am a marsupial.
- Some people think I am a bear.

Crack the code to discover (A) my name and (B) the name of something I like to eat.

**A.** 16  12  26  15  26

**B.** 20  6  14     15  22  26  5  22  8

_ _ _ _ _     _ _ _ _ _ _ _ _

(Hint: A = 26, B = 25, C = 24)

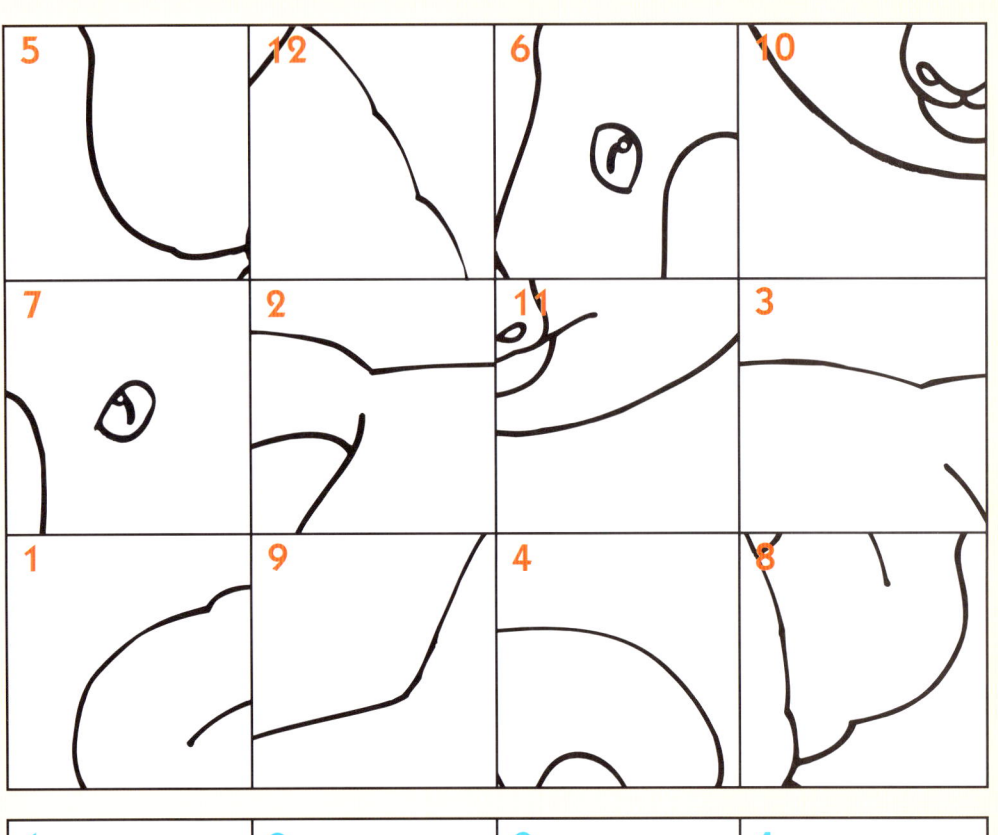

- The top drawing is the mystery animal.
- The grid below has the numbers rearranged in the right order to form the picture.
- Just copy the drawing in each numbered square one at a time to see the whole picture.
- You might like to colour-in your finished drawing.

**DID YOU KNOW?**

This animal is actually awake for just over four hours a day. This means that altogether it is really only awake for less than two and a half days a week.

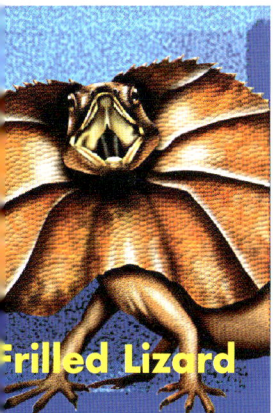
**Frilled Lizard**

**Rainbow Bee-eater**

**Laughing Kookaburra**

**Gouldian Finch**

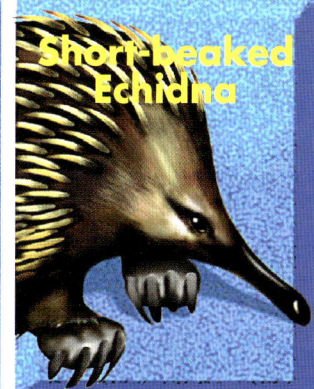
**Short-beaked Echidna**

**Barn owl**

**Quoll**

**Goanna**

**Koala**

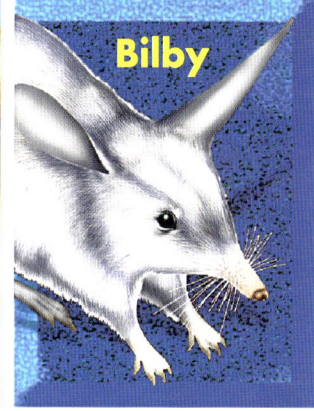
**Bilby**

**Brushtail possum**

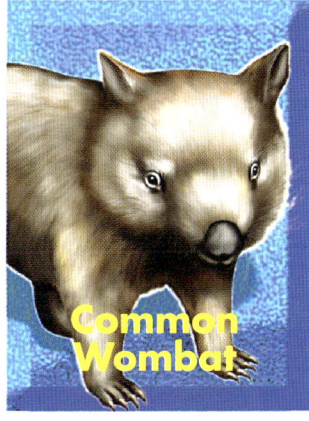
**Common Wombat**

**Galah**

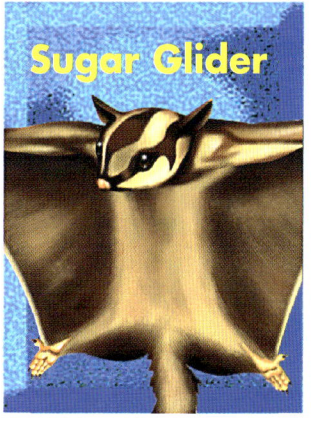
**Sugar Glider**

**Emu**

**Wanderer butterfly**

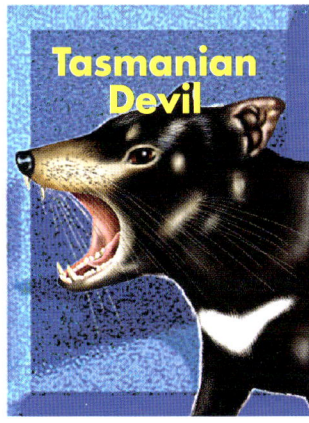
**Tasmanian Devil**

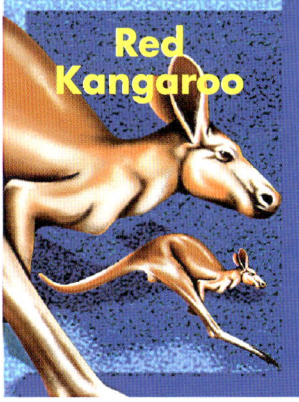
**Red Kangaroo**

**Numbat**

**Dingo**

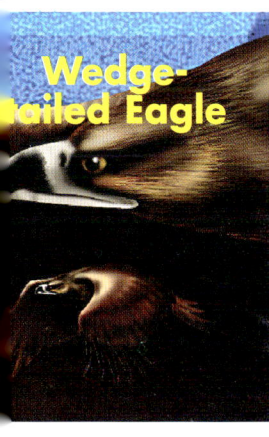
**Wedge-tailed Eagle**

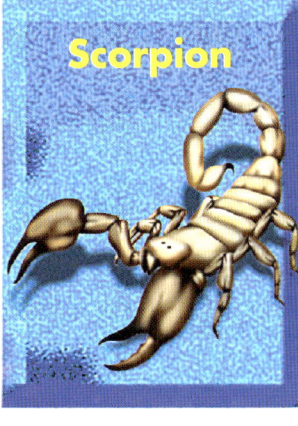
**Scorpion**

**Tiger snake**

**Thorny Devil**

**Christmas beetle**

The echidna is a monotreme, whose young are hatched from an egg. Their spines are an effective means of defence, as echidnas roll into a spiny ball to escape attackers.

Gouldians are the only Australian finches to nest only in tree hollows or termite mounds. Once widespread across tropical northern Australia, their numbers have declined drastically during the twentieth century.

Kookaburras are kingfishers, birds which have large heads and long, strong bills. The Laughing Kookaburra makes a chuckling sound, while the Blue-winged Kookaburra makes a maniacal cackle.

Rainbow Bee-eaters eat wasps, bees and dragonflies. When they catch their prey, they whack it on a branch, work out which end has the sting, and scrape it off against the branch before eating the insect.

The Frilled Lizard is type of lizard known as a dragon. When threatened, this lizard may stand its ground extending the folds of skin around its neck to appear larger and more frightening to its enemies.

Bilbies have long, rabbit-like ears which act as a cooling system. The ears have many blood vessels which, when exposed to the air, cool the animal's blood down as it circulates.

Koalas eat for around 4 hours a day and sleep for just under 20 hours. Their diet of gum leaves generates little energy to move about, so only a small amount of a Koala's time is spent climbing trees or finding a mate.

The name "goanna" comes from the word "iguana" which was originally the Spanish word for lizard *l'iguane*. Goannas are also known as monitors. They have powerful limbs and are excellent climbers.

Quolls are easily recognisable by their spotted backs. The name "quoll" is an Aboriginal word for the Eastern Quoll. The Western Quoll's Aboriginal name is the Chuditch.

Barn owls have heart shaped discs around their dark eyes. They can catch a mouse in total darkness, tracking their victim by sound alone. In dim light their eyes are three times more sensitive than human eyes.

The longest recorded journey by an Emu was 540 kilometres, moving at 13.5 kilometres a day. Sprinting Emus can run at 48 km/h, while an ostrich can do 60 km/h.

Sugar Gliders have a membrane stretching from fore limb to hind limb on each side. This allows them to glide for at least 50 metres from one tree to another.

Galahs, like other cockatoos, are very playful birds and they are fortunate in having benefited from new supplies of grain and water since European settlement, being able to expand their ranges into settled areas.

The wombat is one of the largest burrowing animals in the world. A wombat can sprint at a pace of 40 km/h when startled and if followed into its burrow, the wombat may crush the attacker against one of the walls with its rump.

Brushtail possums are one nocturnal animal often seen by people, even city-dwellers. Outside of bushlands, they live in many city parks and reserves and frequently climb into the ceilings of houses.

The Dingo arrived in Australia only 3500 years ago from South-East Asia and thrived here. After the Dingo's arrival, the Thylacine and the Tasmanian Devil became extinct on mainland Australia.

Although 200 years ago Numbats could be found across the country, today they are endangered and live only in a small area of eucalypt forest in Western Australia.

The Red Kangaroo is the largest kangaroo. Red Kangaroos are capable of hopping at great speed, and one male was timed moving at 56 km/h for 1.6 kilometres.

Tasmanian Devils once existed on mainland Australia as well as Tasmania. Despite its menacing jaws, the Tasmanian Devil is easily defeated by a determined dog and is not a fast runner.

The Wanderer Butterfly arrived in Australia from North America in about 1870. Like the Wanderer, most butterflies rest with their wings held upright over their bodies.

Christmas beetles are familiar to many Australians as they are frequent visitors to many suburban gardens during the summer months. Their metallic colours help to conceal the beetles on shiny leaves.

This scary looking lizard is actually extremely gentle. Thorny Devils can camouflage themselves to blend in with their environment, as they can change their colours and patterns over a period of several hours.

Tiger snakes are venomous snakes known as elapid or front-fanged snakes. They have sharp, hollow fangs at the front of their mouths through which their venom is injected into their victims.

Fossil scorpions date back to 400 million years ago. Scorpions are related to spiders, ticks and mites. They are aggressive and carnivorous, and the sting in their tail can prove extremely painful to humans.

The Wedge-tailed Eagle is a large predator, with a wingspan of up to 2.3 metres. The males perform spectacular aerial courtship rituals to impress the females.

# Doorhangers

STOP
GLUE

### THE DINGO

Dingos don't bark, they howl. It is only when they are continually exposed to the barking of domestic dogs that they can learn how to bark.

HOWL BEFORE ENTERING

## RED KANGAROOS

The Red Kangaroo is the biggest kangaroo of all. Rival male kangaroos sometimes wrestle with each other to fight for dominance.

DON'T BE KANGARUDE PLEASE KNOCK!

# YOU CAN HELP OUR BUSHLAND

In the past 200 years large areas of bushland have been cleared for cities, towns and farms. Weeds, domestic animals gone wild, crops and grazing stock all challenge the survival of bushland plants and animals.

Finding a balance between our needs and those of the natural environment is difficult but not impossible.

Everyone needs to help if we want to preserve our bushland animals and plants.

You could:
- go bushwalking with your family.
- make a list of native animals that visit your garden.
- read more books about the bush.
- join a conservation group.
- grow a gum tree.

# Grow your own
# Gum tree

Gum trees, especially big old ones, are important homes for many animals. They provide food, shelter and nesting places. Growing native trees is one way you can help our bushland animals.

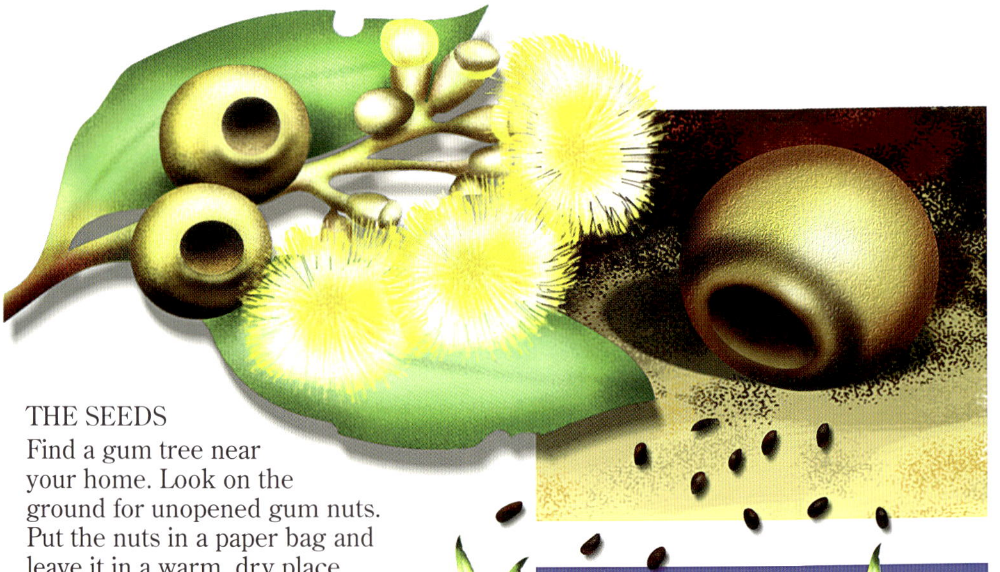

### THE SEEDS
Find a gum tree near your home. Look on the ground for unopened gum nuts. Put the nuts in a paper bag and leave it in a warm, dry place. The nuts will open in about a week. Most seeds are very small and dark in colour.

### PLANTING THE SEEDS
You will need some containers with holes in the bottom. Try take-away or margarine containers. Fill two-thirds of each container with damp potting mix and place them on a tray. Sprinkle the seeds onto the soil and cover them lightly with more soil. Put the tray in a protected spot where it will get the morning sun. Keep the soil damp.

### POTTING THE SEEDLINGS
When the seedlings have their second pair of leaves you can plant each one in a separate 10 cm pot. Later, when the root system has developed, you will need to transfer your plants to 14 cm pots.

### PLANTING OUT
Many gum trees grow too big to be planted in ordinary house gardens. You could plant your trees near where you found the seeds. Autumn and early spring are the best times to plant out your young trees.

Remember, not even nature has a 100% success rate!

### POTTING MIX
You can buy special seed raising mix or make your own with 3 parts coarse sand and 1 part finely powdered peat moss.